SCHIRMER'S LIBRARY OF MUSICAL CLASSICS

Vol. 1737

RODOLPHE KREUTZER

Forty-Two Studies

For the Viola

Transcribed for the Viola and edited by
WALTER BLUMENAU

G. SCHIRMER, *Inc.*

7777 W. BLUEMOUND RD. P.O. BOX 13819 MILWAUKEE, WI 53213

Forty-Two Studies

R. Kreutzer
Transcribed for viola and edited by
Walter Blumenau

u = upper part of bow
l = lower part of bow
WB. = whole bow
A = A-string
D = D-string
G = G-string
C = C-string

I = first position
II = second position
etc.
—— (Dash) = leave the finger on the string to the end of the dash
⊐ = put down the finger in preparation for a note to come

1

Forty varied bowings for the performance of Study No. 2

*Use fingering in parentheses given in Study No. 2

Practise with same bowings as preceding **study**.

4

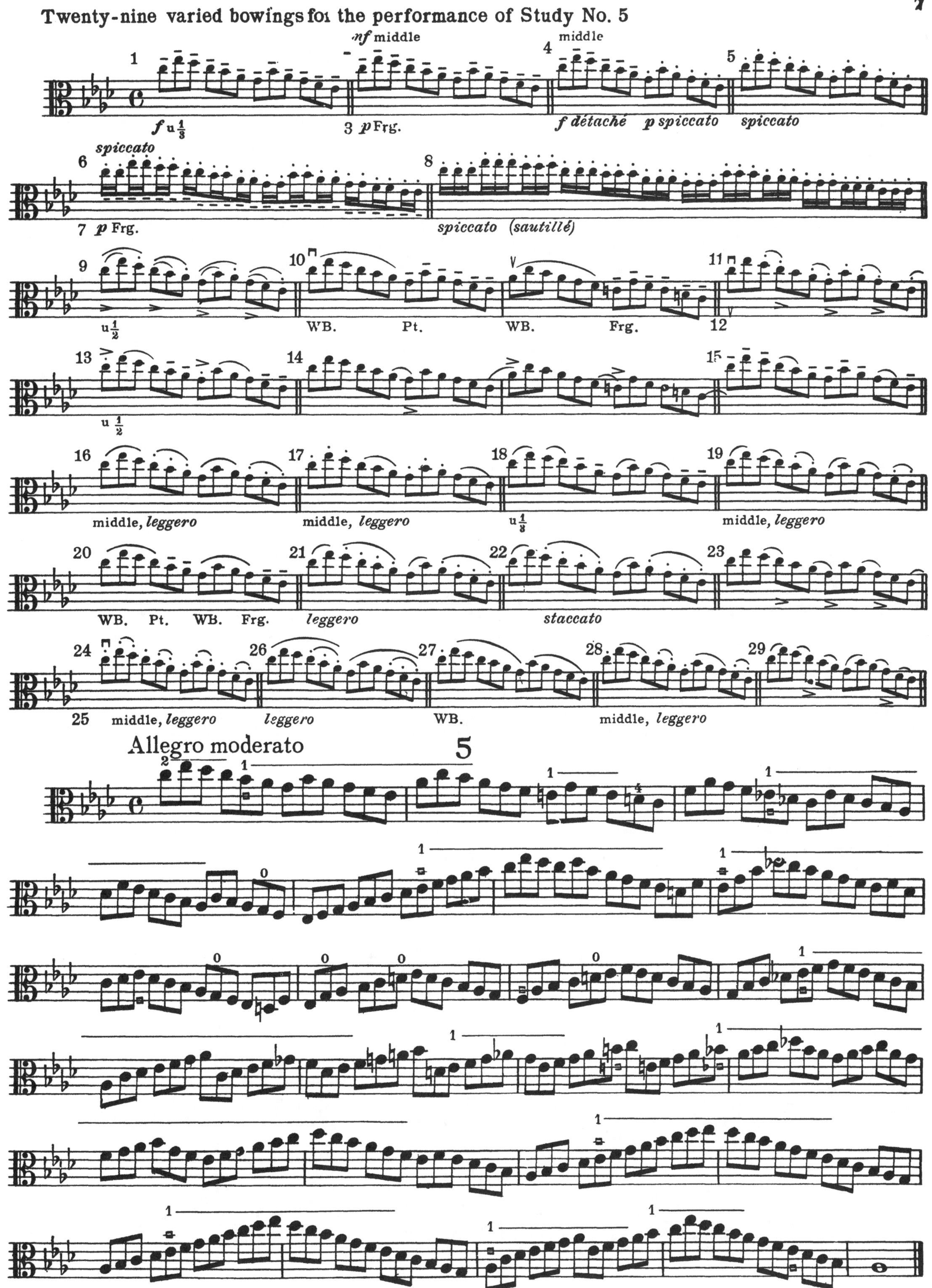
Twenty-nine varied bowings for the performance of Study No. 5
f u 1/3
mf middle
3 p Frg.
middle
f détaché p spiccato
spiccato
spiccato
7 p Frg.
spiccato (sautillé)
u 1/2
WB. Pt. WB. Frg.
middle, leggero
middle, leggero
u 1/3
middle, leggero
WB. Pt. WB. Frg.
leggero
staccato
25 middle, leggero
leggero
WB.
middle, leggero
Allegro moderato
5

6

7

Twenty-four varied bowings for the performance of Study No. 8

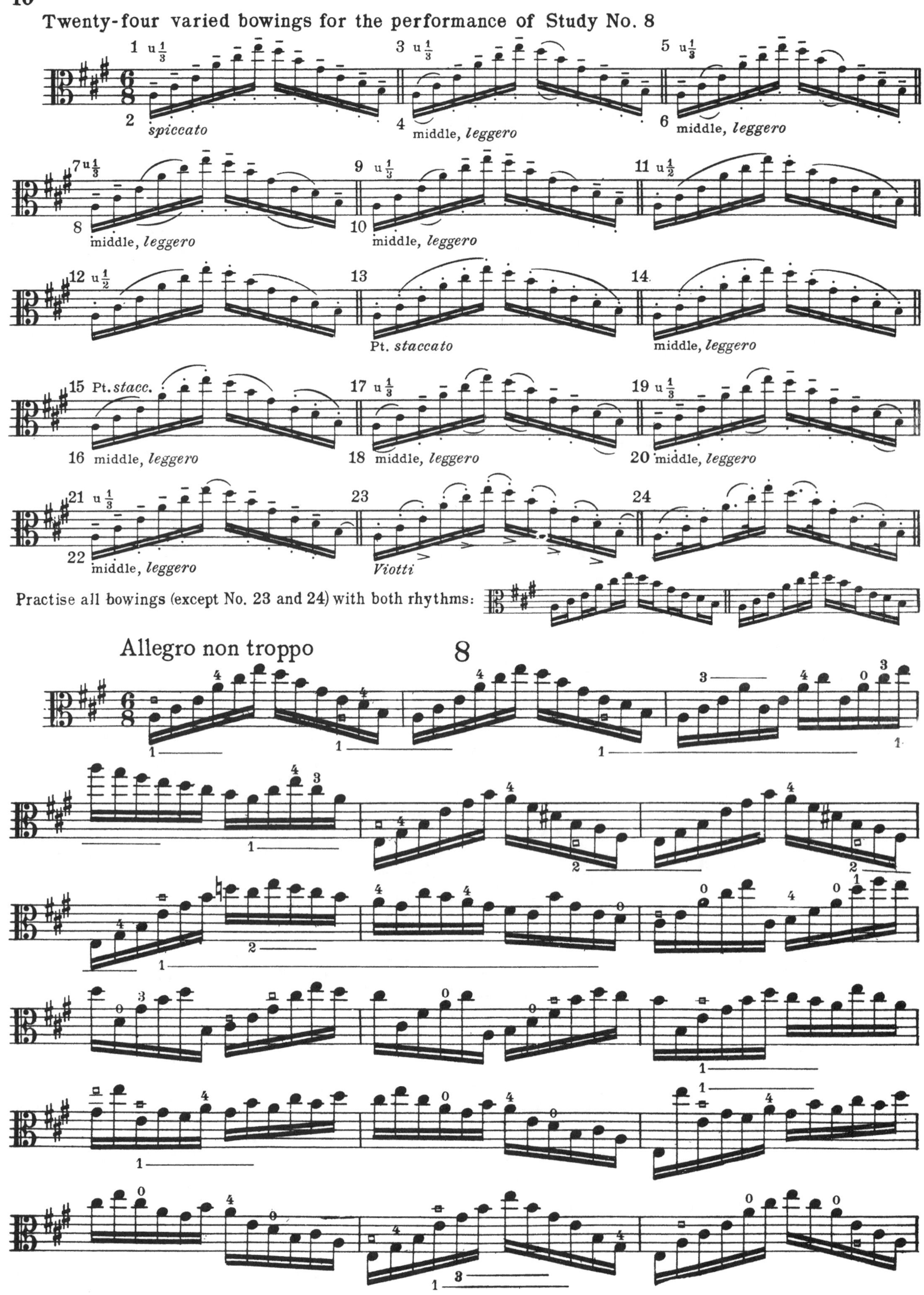

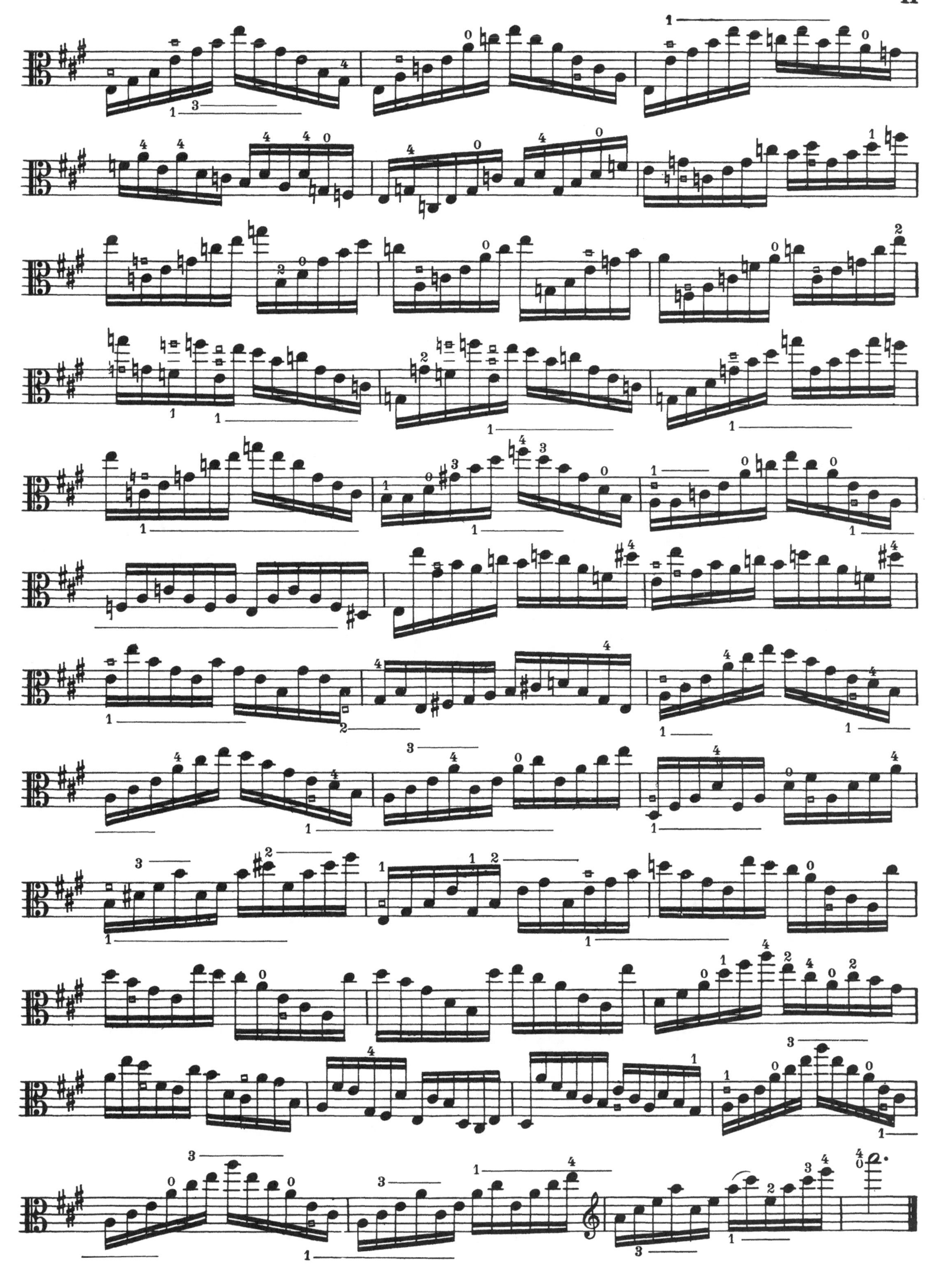

9

10

Andante
WB.
u 1/3
l 1/3
Moderato
Pt.
u 1/2
middle
l 1/2
Frg.
Moderato
segue

11

12

13

Moderato

tr

14

Moderato *(Tranquillo)*

V
I
f
p
tr
III

15
Allegro non troppo (Molto moderato)
segue

16

Editors differ in their rhythmical analyses of the first quarter beat. It is given here in accordance with the notation presented in authentic old editions, and should be practised in that way. The two following variants are also recommended:

*In some editions this rhythm is given:

18

IV
Frg.
détaché
segue

19

20

21
Moderato
marcato
etc.
*In some editions this rhythm is given:

22

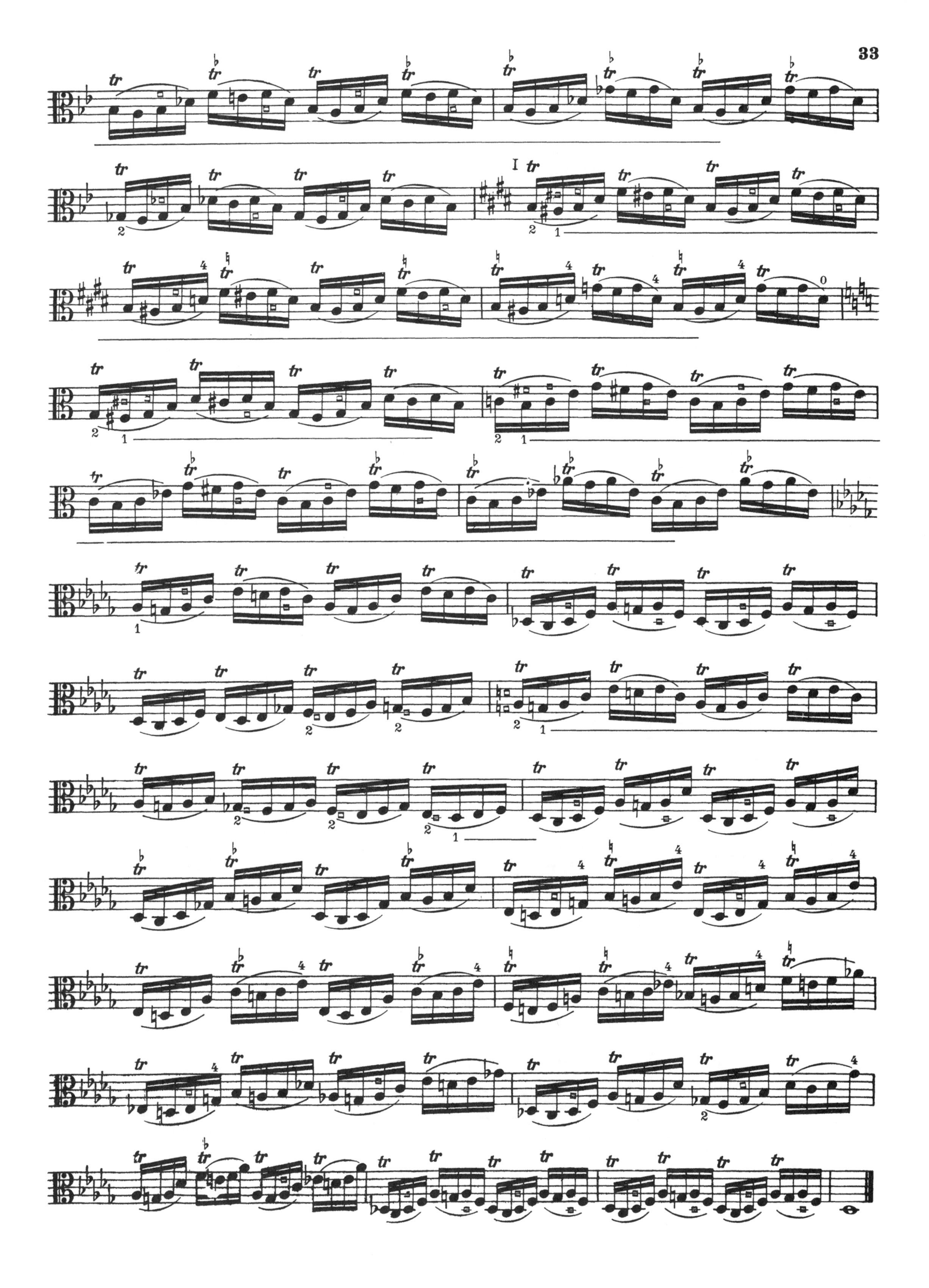

23

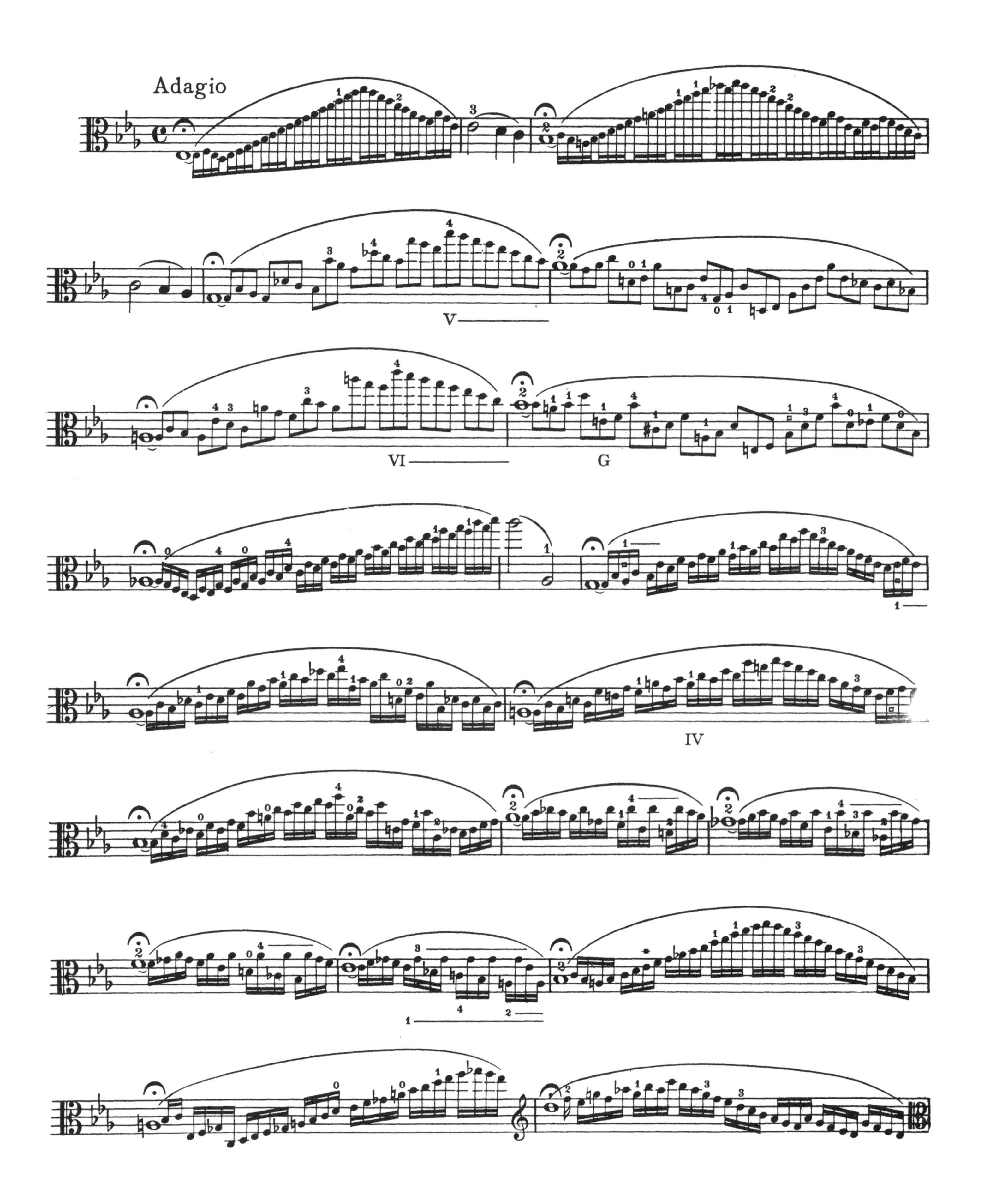

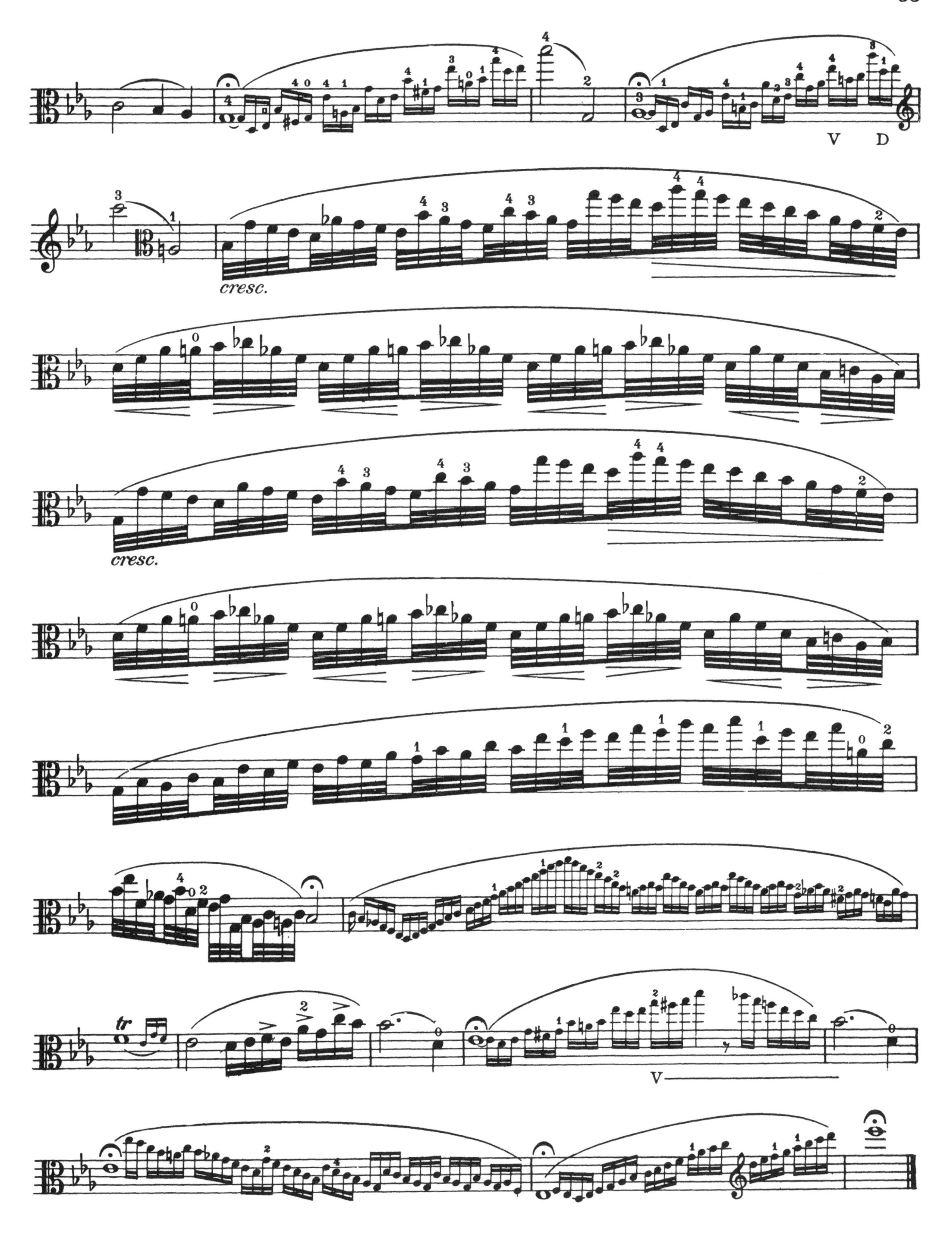
V
D
cresc.
cresc.
tr
V

24

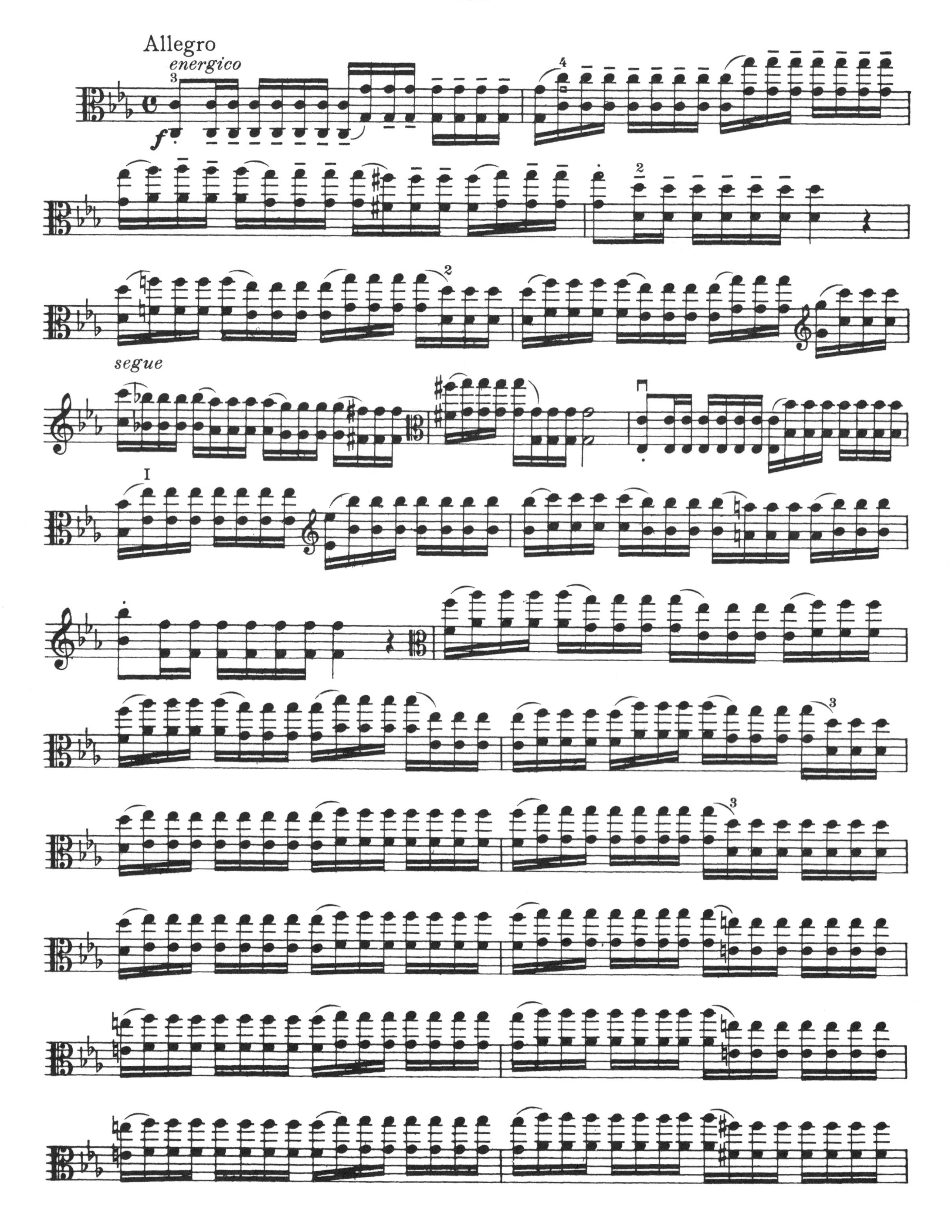

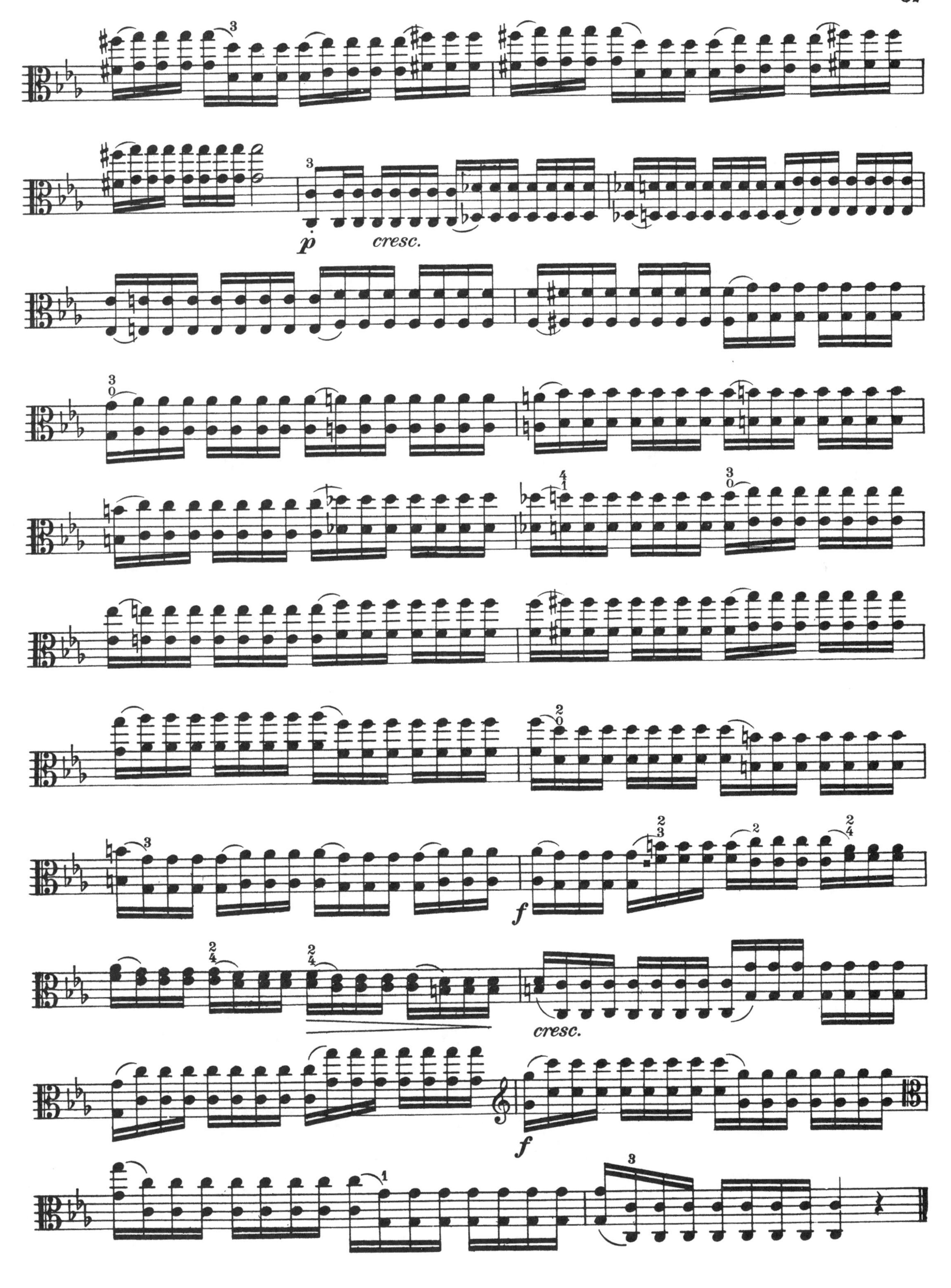
p
cresc.
f
cresc.
f

25

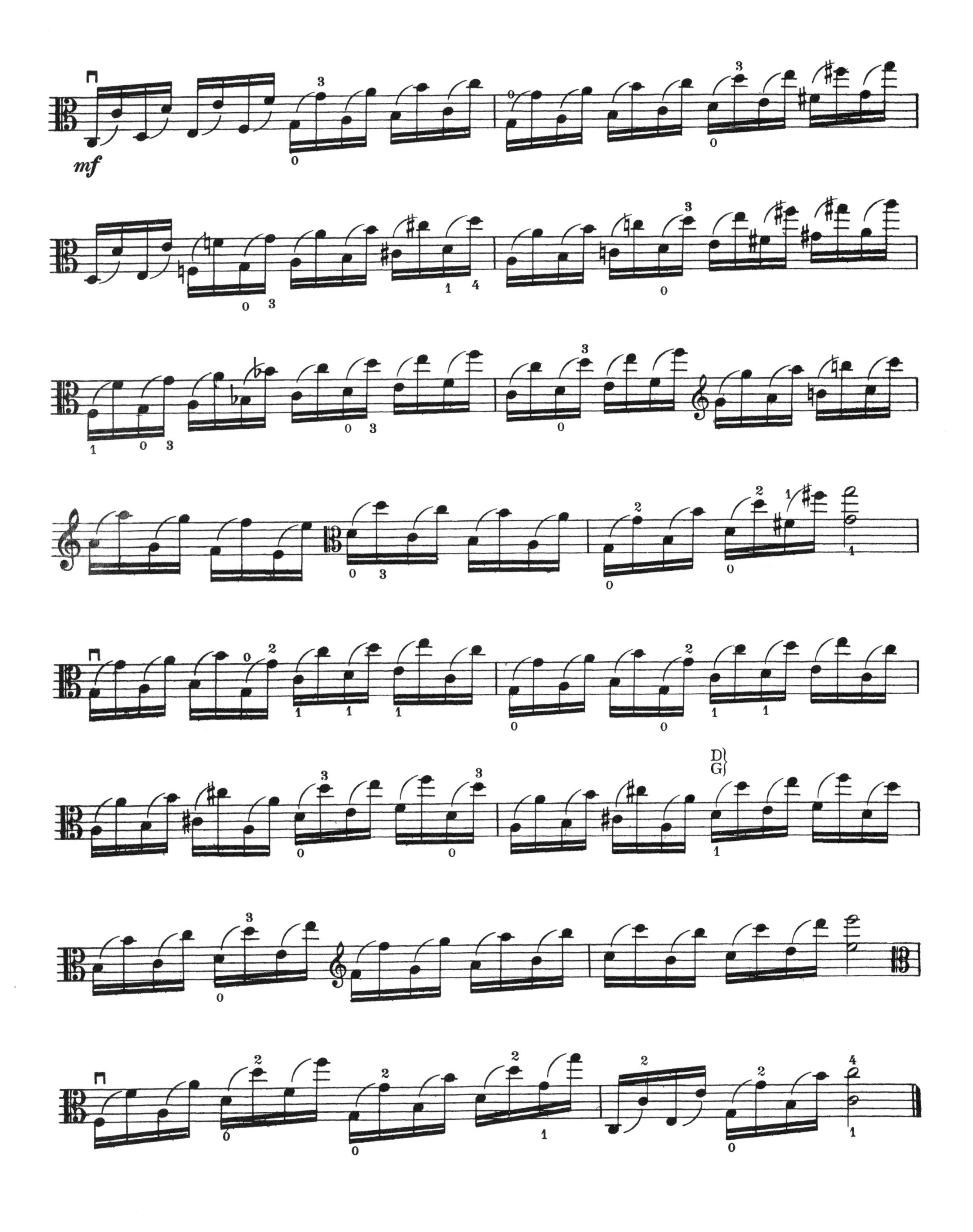

mf
D
G

26

Moderato

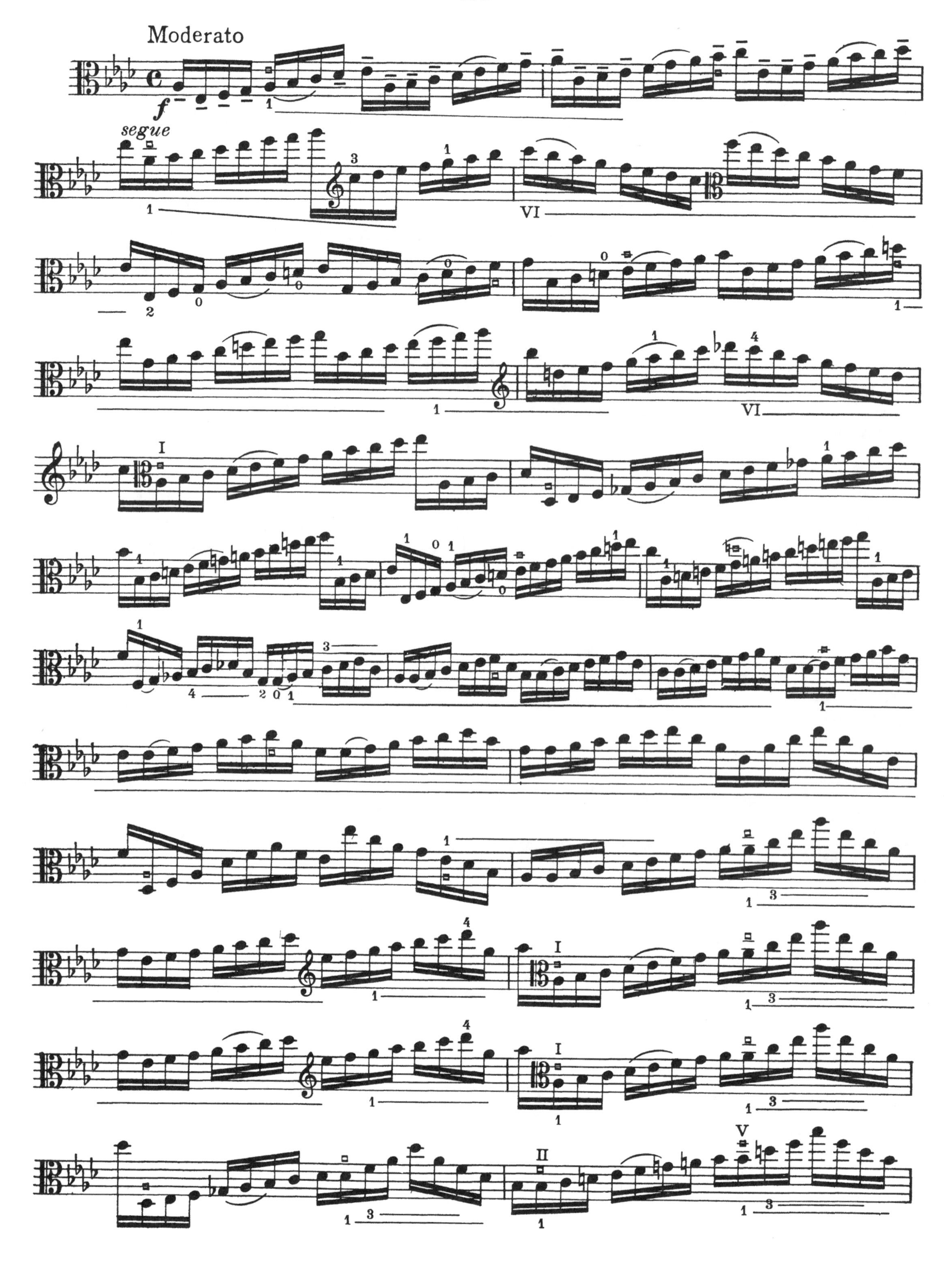

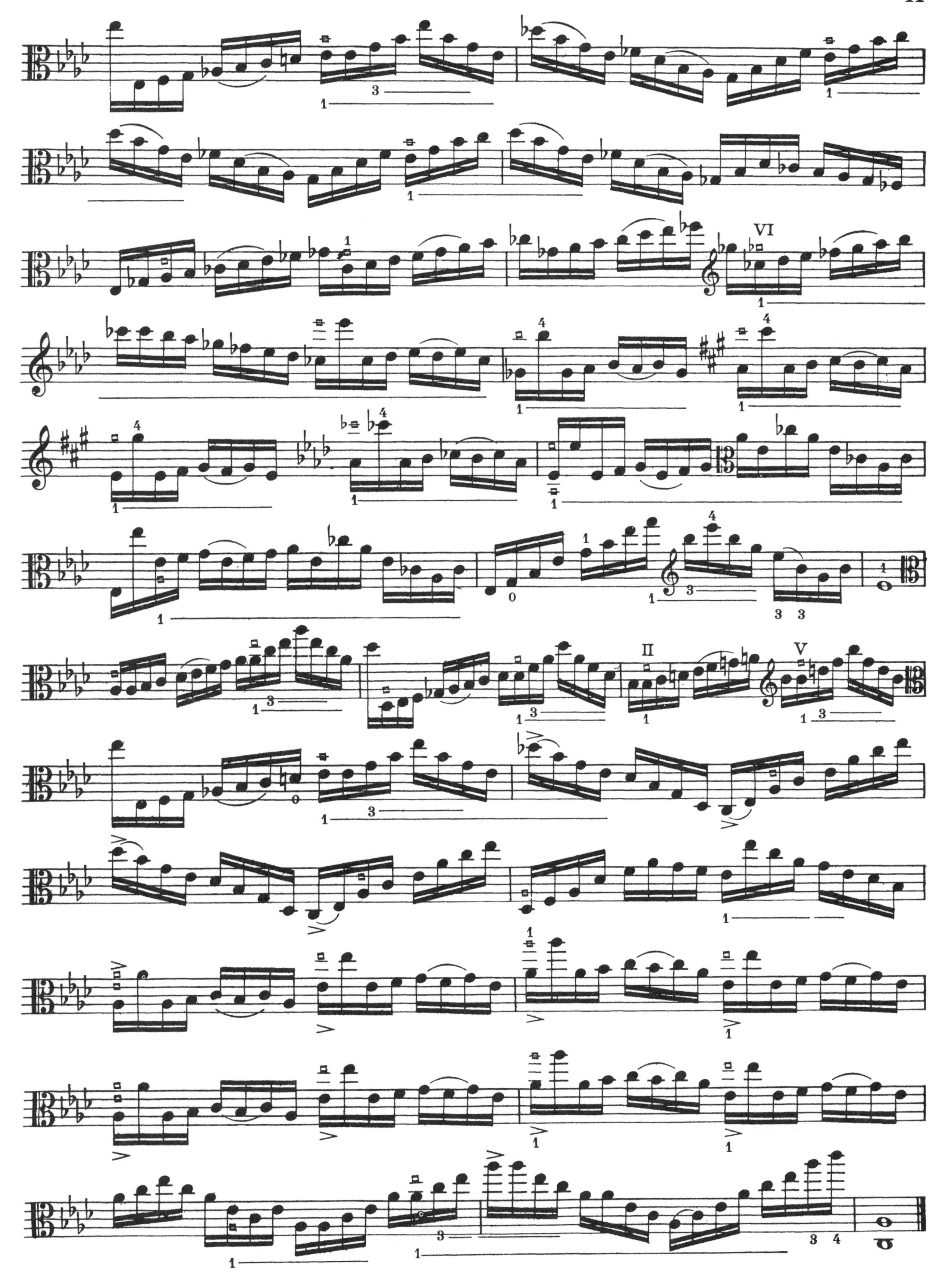
VI
II
V

27

28

Grave
ff
a)
tr
f
p
cresc.
IV
b)
sostenuto
V
VI
a)
Firm staccato at the point.
b)
etc.

ff
f
tr
p sostenuto
I
G

29

30
Moderato

III
WB.

31

tr
I
II
IV

32

33

34

35

March
Allegro maestoso

tr
cresc.
cresc.

36

37

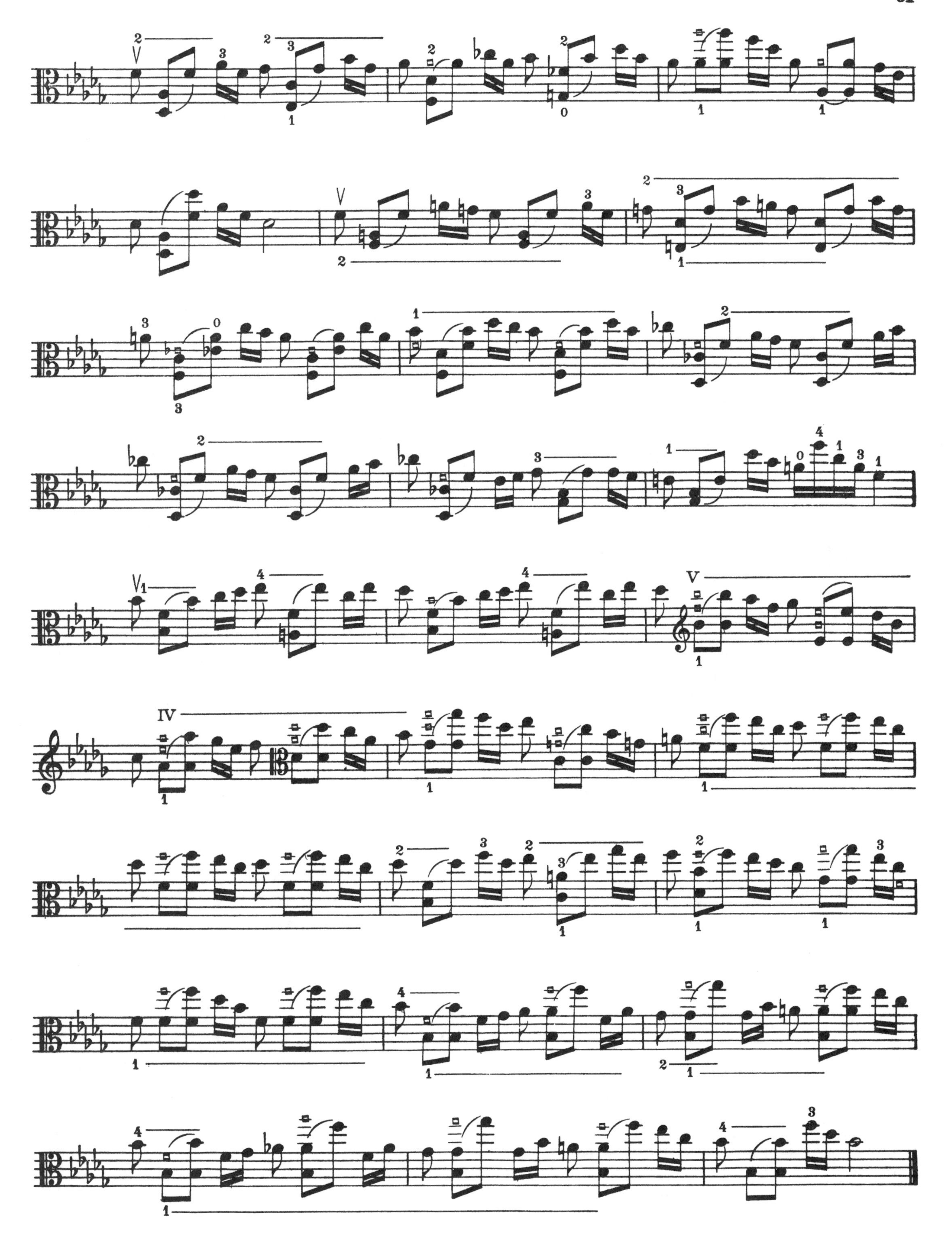

38

39

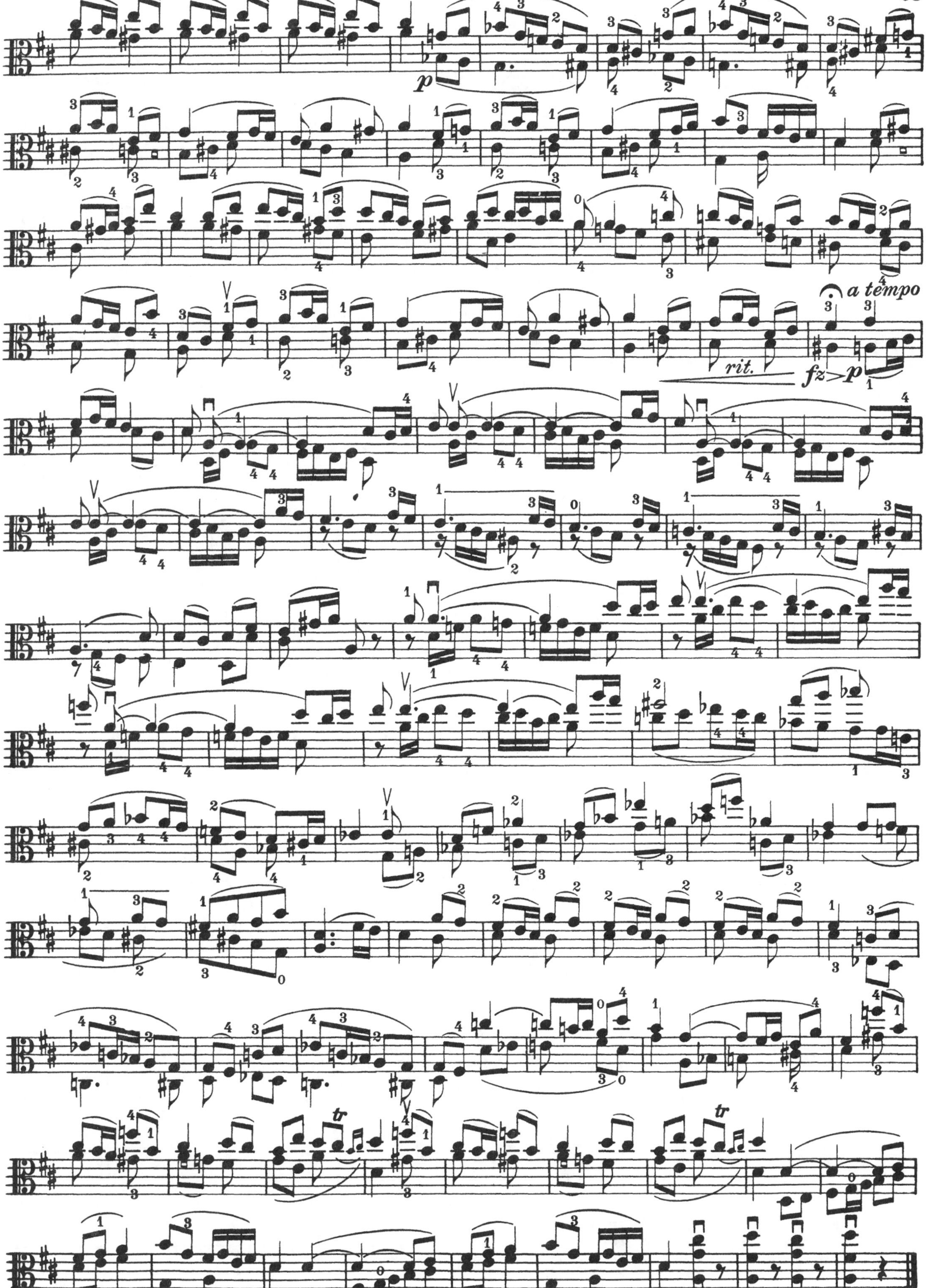
a tempo
rit.
tr

40

Grace note indicates starting trill with upper note.

41

Adagio

42

cre - - - scen - - - - - do
f
allargando